My Husband, My King

A candid and practical
Shalom Bayis Book for Women

DOVID KAPLAN

My Husband, My King:
A candid and practical *Shalom Bayis*
Book for Women

Dovid Kaplan

First Published: September 2020

Copyright © 2019: Adir Press

ISBN: 978-1-988022-56-7

ADIR
PRESS

To discuss publishing your material
— self-publishing or regular publishing —
email: *submissions@AdirPress.com*
or visit us at *www.Adir Press.com*

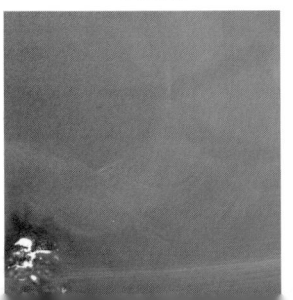

Rabbi Zev Leff

Rabbi of Moshav Matityahu
Rosh HaYeshiva—Yeshiva Gedola Matityahu

בס״ד

הרב זאב לף

מרא דאתרא מושב מתתיהו
ראש הישיבה—ישיבה גדולה מתתיהו

D.N. Modiin 71917   Tel: 08–976–1138 טל'   Fax: 08–976–5326 פקס'   ד.נ. מודיעין 71917

Dear Friends,

I have read the book "My Husband My King" by my esteemed friend and colleague Rabbi Dovid Kaplan.

This is a companion to his book "My Wife My Queen" which deals with the proper manner a husband should relate to his wife. This book deals with the wife's conduct in properly relating to her husband.

Both books convey the foundations of a Jewish marriage as mandated by the Torah and Chazal. These ideas are presented in a straight forward manner with down to earth practical advice and examples.

The basis for a healthy and happy husband wife relationship is mutual respect and consideration and these books are instructive in how to fulfill that mandate in real life situations.

I commend Rabbi Kaplan, who is a top rate educator and counselor, with a quality presentation. I recommend these books respectively to husbands and wives who wish to enhance their sholom bayis and introduce more of the bliss of G-d's presence into their marriage.

I pray that Hashem Yisborach bless Rabbi Kaplan and his family with life, health and the wherewithal to continue to merit Klal Yisroel in his many and varied ways.

Sincerely,
With Torah blessings

Zev Leff

Rabbi Zev Leff

Publisher's Preface

After the tremendous success of Rabbi Dovid Kaplan's first book on marriage, My Wife, My Queen, intended for the husband, Rabbi Kaplan has completed the set by focusing, this time, on the wife's role in marriage. In My Husband, My King — his third book for Adir Press — Rabbi Kaplan has come once again with experience, humor and insight to drive home clear and simple messages that are guaranteed to have a lasting impact on one's marriage.

The meaning of "shalom bayis" is not merely as its literal translation suggests. A "home of shalom" is not simply a "peaceful home" where there are no arguments and everyone just gets along with each other. Rather, a home of "shalom" is a home of "shleimus" — a home of "perfection", where two people — two parts of the same soul — can literally complete each other by fulfilling the other's lack, as well as helping to build and guide their partner in this world.

The verse in Mishlei associates a good wife with goodness itself (18:22). There is no greater good than shalom, as the final Mishnah in the Shas says: Hashem could not find a vessel to contain blessing to Israel besides shalom (Mishnayos Uktzin 3:12). This book, therefore, has lofty goals, but with Hashem's help, will guide and build those who read it.

My sincere prayer is that in every home, this book — together with its counterpart — is read, learned and implemented in the correct way, and that Hashem bestows His blessing of shalom to every bayis.

Rabbi Moshe Kormornick
Adir Press

Acknowledgements

It is with much gratitude to HaKadosh Baruch Hu that we present this book to the English-speaking public.

I wish to thank Rav Zev Leff for taking the time to review the book and honor me with his approbation.

Special thanks to Rabbi Moshe Kormornick and his staff at Adir Press for their professionalism and pleasantness, which have made it a pleasure to work with them.

Most of all I must thank my wife, who, in spite of my shortcomings has always made me feel like a king. The novelty of marriage was finding out that a king must sometimes take orders too — and for that I thank her even more.

Dovid Kaplan

Table of Contents

Introduction

The *sefer Menoras HaMa'or* quotes a Medrash regarding a girl who was about to get married and was given advice by her mother. "If you act as a servant and treat him as a king," she said, "then he'll act as a servant and treat you as royalty. But, if you lord yourself over him, he'll treat you as a servant."

The title of this book, *My Husband, My King*, is taken from that story, as is the title of the companion volume for men, *My Wife, My Queen*. As I wrote in the introduction to the men's volume, the primary responsibility when it comes to shalom bayis (peace in the home) lies with the husband. However, there are also areas that a wife must always be focused on, and doing so will help ensure that there is harmony in the home, which brings in its wake the presence of the *Shechinah* (Divine Presence).

This book is thicker than the men's book for several reasons, none of which is that the wife is more responsible for shalom in the home than her husband. Rather, I have found that women have more patience to read in general and are willing to spend more time focused on marriage. In addition, the nature of marriage is such that the husband does quantifiably less for the wife than the wife does for the husband. As the one in charge of domestics, she has more things that she generally provides the husband with, such as meals, laundry, etc., whereas he is usually more responsible for one big thing, which is *parnassah*. Incidentally, this is the case even if the wife is the primary breadwinner, because at the end of the day , when push comes to shove, the responsibility to ensure that finances are taken care of is his, as is clearly written in the *kesubah* (marital contract) that he gave her on their wedding day.

So, whereas the men's book focuses for the most part on how a man must *treat* his wife, this volume is heavy on what a wife *should do* for her husband. The reason for this is that, as mentioned, the nature of each spouse's job description by definition creates a situation where the wife engages in more activities for the benefit of her husband, and it is her coming up short in what he perceives as his needs that primarily causes the shalom bayis issues that the wife is responsible for. On the other hand, the husband, who is out of the home more, has a responsibility to treat his wife with respect and sensitivity, and it is usually the failure of the husbands in these areas that create problems.

There is also a stylistic difference between the two books. The men's book is very direct, with much more emphasis on the "what" over the "why." This volume is much softer in style and is more focused on the "why."

Of course, not everything written in this book applies to all marriages, but as you read through it you'll most like-

ly find that quite a bit does apply to yours. Please take out of this book those points that can help improve your marriage. Even great marriages can become better.

It is likely that at some point while reading this book you will think to yourself, *But isn't my husband supposed to* . . . or *Shouldn't my husband have to* . . . or something along those lines. Your thoughts are probably correct, but please keep in mind that this book is addressing the ladies. The men's book tells the husbands — in quite a frank, clear, and sometimes even harsh manner — what is expected of them.

I was once in the office of a dental technician who manufactured false teeth and dentures. He had a sign hanging on his wall that said, "Only floss those teeth you want to keep." *Chazal* say, "A kosher woman is one who does the will of her husband" (*Tanna D'Vei Eliyahu Rabbah*, 9). This book is written for those ladies who wish to fulfill this dictum of *Chazal* to the fullest. As a rule, when it comes to any sort of *mussar* books or books on self-improvement, ironically, the less you feel you need it, the more you probably do.

Some of the ideas in this book may repeat themselves because in various areas of life, the same underlying problem may be relevant. So, for example, if there is friction with regard to how money should be spent, the underlying cause may be the same as the reason there is stress when dealing with the kids. That being the case, the same ideas may appear in the book a number of times.

I have tried to incorporate real-life scenarios and examples so that the ideas presented become more concrete. These are by no means all-inclusive — there are simply too many life situations to possibly cover every single one. I have also not addressed every area of marriage — far from it. That is a virtual impossibility due to the multifaceted nature of marriage. What I have tried to do is cover very common areas of marital challenge, and hopefully the ideas presented will then serve as a foundation and springboard to be implemented in other areas as well.

For the sake of readability, you will find that sometimes I have written in second person ("you should") and sometimes in third person ("a wife should," "one should").

There are a lot of excellent marriage books out there, so what need is there for another? I've noticed that most of the books written for women have been written by women. While they may have an excellent understanding of men, I have actually lived as one my entire life, which allows me to present a perspective that comes not only from understanding but from actual experience. As such, there are points in this book that a woman, regardless of how perceptive she is, is unlikely to be able to tap into.

One last note: There are many ideas in this book regarding what a wife's obligations and responsibilities are. In many of the cases, a considerate husband should and often will ignore what she should be doing because he himself is working on his obligation to be a considerate husband. As a wife, you should be thinking about what *you* must do without thinking, *If he would only work on himself I wouldn't have to be doing this.*

The story is told about an older couple that was having a fiftieth wedding anniversary celebration. All their children and grandchildren were there, and a caterer provided a delectable meal. One of the waiters approached the head table, where the husband and wife were sitting, and asked what they'd like. The wife chose a piece of dark chicken.

One of the grandchildren who happened to be next to them asked, "Bubby, why are you taking the dark chicken? Every time we've been over for Shabbos you always take the white part."

"The truth is," Bubby answered, "I prefer dark meat. But I know that Zaidy prefers the dark meat, so for fifty years I've been eating the white."

"Well, I actually prefer the *white* meat," Zaidy interjected, "and for fifty years I've been taking the dark meat because I thought you liked the white meat."

No one said anything for a moment.

"Then I guess you *both* lost," said the grandchild.

"No," they answered in unison, with big smiles on their faces. "We both *won*."

The goal of this book and the accompanying men's volume is that you and your husband should be able to look back and realize that the giving, sacrifices, and everything else you do for each other have made you winners — the biggest winners possible in the most important area of life.

Dovid Kaplan

CHAPTER 1

Chessed Begins at Home

Most of us are familiar with the expression "Charity begins at home." The Torah has a similar view on the subject. *Chessed* (kindness) is a series of concentric circles. That means the first priority is one's inner circle, specifically one's husband and children. Next on the list is extended family, followed by close friends, and then extending further outward. If there is a conflict between two opportunities or obligations to do *chessed*, one should follow that order if he or she desires to do the will of Hashem.

Of course, if one is outside the home anyhow and a *chessed* situation arises, for example, helping an old lady carry her packages, one should grab the opportunity. However, if there is a *conflict* between what one would like to do versus what one should do, "should do" always trumps "like to do."

So for example, you've been asked to bake a cake for an engagement party for someone you know. The problem is there's a conflict between that and getting your husband's supper ready. You may be thinking, *Well, I guess he'll have salami sandwiches just this one time,* or, *I'll make him an omelet.* But the correct thing to do if you can't do both is to prioritize your husband. The person who asked you to bake has to be told that you won't be able to get to it. Of course, if you know for certain — and I mean for absolutely *certain* — that your husband would rather you do the *chessed* outside the home and he'll eat cold food, then it's fine. But if he isn't OK with it, even if he controls himself and doesn't show any anger or signs of being upset, caring for others is not the correct thing to do.

The argument that "he can eat a sandwich one night" is not valid for two reasons: First of all, he should never be the casualty of your *chessed* unless it is with his express approval. It is for this reason that a woman is for the most part exempt from the mitzvah of honoring her parents if it conflicts with her marital duties. Second of all, the engagement party can take place with cakes purchased from a store; it's not as if your contribution is a matter of life or death. So why should your husband's preference be sacrificed for the sake of someone else's?

Again, and I will repeat this several times in the book, a husband, for his part, must work on himself to not be too limiting and demanding on his wife. But that is *his* responsibility — which those who have read the book for men are well aware of if they weren't before. This book is for the ladies, and as such the focus is on what your priorities should be.

Another example: Your husband asked you before he left the house to mend a couple of pairs of pants that need repair because he's running low. You were about to get to it when someone called and told you that an old, unmarried friend from your seminary years is visiting in the neighborhood and could really use a listening ear — which you are really good at providing — for some issues she has. As important as that is, your husband's wishes come first, and if there's a conflict, she will need to have someone else provide that ear.

A very common source of conflict of interests is when the wife wants to have guests, either because she feels it's an important mitzvah or because she feels it's more interesting when it's not just the immediate family, but the husband would really like to have a quiet Shabbos. It may even be that he wants to have quiet Shabbosim on a regular basis. A good wife must set aside her preference for the sake of her husband.

A man in his seventies told me that he likes to have some serenity on Shabbos once in a while without all the tumult that comes from having his grandchildren there. His wife refuses. "I *have to have* at least one of the families and their kids here every Shabbos," she told him. This is a classic example of a woman who is doing what *she* wants — but not what Hashem wants of her.

This sort of thing may also come up when it comes to taking care of the kids. You get a call that someone needs you for something — perhaps an old lady in a nursing home would like a bit of company — and you decide to run over. However, this means your husband will have to watch the kids, something he may not be in the mood to do just then. Or it could be that he needs to leave soon for *Maariv* (the evening prayer) or a night *chavrusa* (study partner). So your mitzvah is coming at the expense of what *he* needs. The argument that "they're his kids too" or "it wouldn't be so bad if he'd spend a bit more time with the children" is irrelevant. That isn't the issue right now, and it likely wouldn't have come up had you not gotten the call. If it was truly an issue that needed fixing, you would have brought it up at a different time. The only issue now is: Do you do what *you* want, or do you do what your husband wants?

One more example, and an extreme one at that: Your husband comes in late Thursday night after his *chavrusa* and starts foraging in the fridge to find something to eat. Women have an ability — men are flabbergasted by it — to be in a deep sleep yet hear a husband by the fridge. Accordingly, you crone from your bed, "Don't take the kuuugggellll! It's for the Feldmans' kiddush this Shabbos." Now, due to this amazing ability, this probably would have happened if Adam had been the one to reach for the forbidden fruit and Chavah had been sleeping. Anyhow, the question is, what should you, the wife — not what *would* you but what *should* you — do at this point? By now I'm sure you know the answer. Your husband should be allowed to get at the kugel, and you'll make another one for the kiddush in the morning. If worst comes to worst, you'll buy one for the kiddush. I repeat yet again, the considerate husband should back off and eat some tuna with crackers, but that's *his* responsibility. The choice of doing the right wifely thing is yours.

CHAPTER 2

Encouragement

There are very few people in the world who don't need encouragement, regardless of what they are involved in trying to accomplish. When it comes to husbands, whether in *ruchni* (spiritual) or *gashmi* (physical) pursuits, encouragement and compliments are needed, and to a certain extent the success of the endeavors is very much dependent on them.

Let's take a look at the *ruchni* aspect first. Many ladies have heard at some time or another during their school or seminary years that "you are not your husband's *mashgiach*." As a *mashgiach*, I disagree with this for a number of reasons. First of all, when you hear the word "*mashgiach*" you probably envision a man in a blue uniform blowing a whistle or arresting someone who has broken the law. You are not at fault for this, because the role of a *mashgiach* may have never been explained to you. People think of a *mashgiach* primarily as a disciplinarian, and therein lies the misunderstanding. A *mashgiach* has several roles, only one of which is enforcing discipline. Another role is providing encouragement and guidance to his charges, which is probably a more important role and has longer-lasting positive effects.

That being the case, you most certainly *should* be your husband's *mashgiach*. You should encourage him constantly regarding his learning, *middos* (character traits) development, davening (praying), and a host of other things that make up a man's growth and progress in *ruchniyus* (spirituality). A man who hears from his wife, "I'm really impressed with how you make it to minyan (congregation of ten or more men for prayer) every morning" is likely to make more of an effort if necessary with the knowledge that his wife notices his efforts.

The same goes for learning, controlling his anger, being willing to spend money, and any other area you could think of. "Wow, you're so easy when it comes to money, Hershel!" will make him feel good. "It's really amazing how you control your anger when there are things that you could get upset about" is not only something he deserves to hear, it will also motivate him to continue with his self-control in the future. Just think how important it is to you to hear that your efforts have been noticed and appreciated.

The area where this is probably most important is Torah learning. Telling your husband enthusiastically how impressed you are with his commitment to learning, regardless of whether he's in *kollel* (yeshivah for married men) full-time or a working man who goes to a *daf yomi shiur* (Torah lesson in the daily page of Gemara), coupled with words indicating your appreciation for the *ruchniyus* he brings into the home, may be the most potent thing you can do to motivate him regarding Torah study.

You should demonstrate appreciation in tangible ways. For example, when he comes home late from his night *seder* (learning session), it would be a good idea to have a fresh pie waiting for him, accompanied by a note that says, "This is to show you how much I appreciate the *ruchniyus* you bring into the home with your learning." Or, if you are trying to show that you notice his efforts at self-improvement, you can write, "This is just to show you that your behavior is as sweet as a pie." Corny? So what? I don't think you'd object to him doing something corny to show his appreciation for you, right?

Now, I want to make something very clear. I'm not referring here to gratitude. Saying thank-you is basic *derech eretz* (common decency), and that is not something I think too many wives need to be reminded about. If they need to be reminded to show gratitude, it's about saying thank-you for things they *wouldn't* think of, such as when he clears off the dishes or goes shopping, things the wife may see as his basic duties.

What I'm talking about is encouragement and compliments. Here's an idea: Make a list of about twenty or thirty adjectives, such as "amazing," "terrific," "wonderful," "awe-inspiring," and so on, and look it over once in a while so that these words are at your command. I'll even help you out and give you a list to start with: Amazing, awesome, awe-inspiring, brilliant, clever, considerate, calm, delicious (as in "You have delicious *middos*!"), exceptional, fantastic, funny, great, heavenly, levelheaded, majestic, magnanimous, neat, organized, polite, patient, quality, regal, remarkable, stable, social, super, terrific, unbelievable, virtuous, wise, witty, ze best. I can almost guarantee you that your usage of any one of these words at any time will improve your husband's mood and behavior. It certainly won't affect him in any negative way. Keep in mind that your husband may not show that it means anything to him, nevertheless, I can almost guarantee that it does.

It should become second nature for you to shower you husband regularly with a variety of adjectives. Men also enjoy — perhaps "melt" is a better word — when a wife says, "I'm so *proud* of you." Ironically, women often find it easier and more natural to praise and compliment just about anyone else in the world — their kids, friends, and even sister-in-law — than they do their husbands. Some ladies wonder, "Is he a little kid that he needs to hear praise? I mean, I *married* him so that he should learn . . ." or "*Any* responsible man supports his family." The response to this is that he isn't a little kid — he's a human being with very normal human needs.

For those who still have trouble with this, simply keep in mind that while he isn't a little kid per se, you should treat him in this regard as if he is. And once again, the same way you crave to hear good things from him, he craves to hear them from you. Maybe on some emotional level there's a difference and the ladies need to hear these things more often, but let's not go there. Just please use the gift of speech that Hashem gave you to pick your husband up and help him achieve the potential you saw in him when you said yes to his marriage proposal.

Here's a wonderful piece of advice: If the two of you are chatting and you have nothing to talk about, talk about him. Liberally apply those adjectives you've committed to memory. While you should do it without ulterior motives, there is a side benefit: if you feel you'd like to hear some good things about yourself, it's almost inevitable that you'll hear them if you start by saying nice things about him.

All of the above applies to when the husband is more or less living up to his wife's expectations. On the other hand, one of the most common questions asked to *rabbanim* by wives is how to get their husband motivated when he isn't doing what he should be. A man may rarely go to minyan, almost never open a *sefer* (holy book), spend way too much time in front of his computer, and so on. Experience shows that nagging and unpleasantness don't usually accomplish much. In some cases nothing will help, and usually in those marriages some sort of professional intervention is required. However, for the average marriage, the surest technique to get a husband moving is: whenever he *does* something he should, the wife should lay it on thick about how proud and impressed she is. There may be only small steps toward improvement, but each and every one should be noticed and commented on, along with some sort of tangible reward. If it doesn't help, it certainly won't hurt.

One last point, going back to that *mashgiach* thing. Every man needs accountability, and you're the one he's accountable to. So, if you do notice him slacking off in his *ruchniyus*, you certainly have to step in to disciplinary *mashgiach* mode. However, this must be done with lots of tact and forethought.

If, for example, you notice your husband is going to shul late on a regular basis, you can ask him if there are any problems in shul. He'll get the message that you've noticed without it coming across as criticism. The same goes for a man who stops going out to his nightly learning session. In some cases you'll discover that there is some sort of issue, like a participant who keeps sidetracking the *shiur* or a feeling of being unwelcome in the shul. Then the two of you could discuss it and deal with it. In some cases — and you must use wisdom and discretion, and a lot depends on how strong the marriage is — you can be a bit more direct and indicate that you think he could be doing better in a particular area. Lots of thought should go into when to say it and how to say it, and perhaps most importantly, whether to say it at all.

CHAPTER 3

Dealing with His Anger

This section deals with one of the most delicate and tricky areas in marriage.

I get called on a regular basis by people who wish to inquire about *bachurim* (young, unmarried men) for *shidduch* (matchmaking) purposes. One of the most frequently asked questions, usually early on, is "Does he get angry?" My response is almost always, "Of course — don't you? Do you know anyone who doesn't?" I then go on to say, if applicable to the boy in question, that I have never seen him lose his temper, or if more accurate, that I have rarely seen it. "If you mean is he the type who will throw chairs when he gets angry, no, I don't think he's that type of guy" is usually how I conclude. The reason I do this is to communicate that looking for a *bachur* who won't get angry after marriage is unrealistic. The question should be asked as "Is he the type who will be explosive when angry?" or "Do you think he'll get angry frequently?" That he won't get angry *ever* — forget about it.

So what can or should a wife do when her husband gets angry? The first thing is to determine what he's really angry about. When a person becomes disproportionately upset about something, like a husband who blows up because someone left a light on, it's likely that something else is really bothering him. It can be a setback at work, a major headache, supper not ready, or coming home to a wife who's in a slovenly or disheveled state. The existing irritability is brought to a head by some little thing, and then the volcano erupts. Once he's been fed and calmed down and is in a more communicative mood, you can find out what the underlying issue is and deal with it.

Your role in avoiding these outbursts is to make every effort to avoid those triggers that experience has shown set him off. Make sure dinner is ready, put yourself together before he arrives, hide all new bills until after he's eaten, and don't spend money irresponsibly. Please understand, I'm not in any way justifying a husband's temper tantrums or outbursts. On the other hand, if you know that there are certain triggers, try to get them taken care of so that his area of vulnerability will not be tested.

"Eliyahu, don't get angry, but . . ." begins wife Nechama. Just about every husband who's been married for any great length of time, like about ten minutes, knows that this introduction means he now has less money than he did previously. The wife may have carelessly broken something expensive, gotten a parking ticket, or otherwise found out about some expense that will put a dent in her husband's wallet. Indeed, money matters are probably the single biggest cause of marital strife and a man's anger.

The first rule is: when reporting unpleasant news, get to the point quickly. A husband senses what's coming, and all he wants at that point is to know what the damage is.

Rule number two is: try as hard as possible to be careful when it comes to appliances and other items that can be damaged.

Rule number three: avoid spending on things that haven't been agreed upon in advance. This doesn't mean the husband gets to make the decisions, it just means you should present your spending wishes before carrying them out, and then the two of you should amicably reach a decision the same way you reach decisions on all matters.

Another trigger for a husband is when he's been making a conscious effort to work on his anger, and then something unpleasant happens and you begin with "Don't get angry, but . . ." The reason this can set him off is that it makes it seem like you haven't noticed his efforts in this area and you are still ready for an explosion. This should not be underestimated; it can really cause a blowup.

As I mentioned earlier, a man is in a better mood when his wife looks her best. An unkempt, kvetchy wife reporting a financial setback is much more likely to hear some hollering than an upbeat wife who is put together. No guarantee, but it's worth taking a shot at it.

Another point: When your husband is upset about something, whether from outside or inside the home, don't downplay it. No one likes to feel that the thing they're upset about is trivial. The first thing you should do is try to understand where he's coming from and empathize. Later, when he's in a better mood, you can discuss whether not getting a promotion or toothpaste squeezed improperly is really such a big deal. Please bear in mind that there are plenty of things you get upset about that your husband sees as trivialities, yet you expect him to understand you, empathize, and certainly not downplay your feelings. You also should never try to calm him while he's in the middle of a tantrum (even a mild one). The best policy when a husband is hollering is to remain silent. If relevant, fix up whatever it is he's upset about, and only much later bring up the issue for review.

In any successful marriage there must be good communication. If your husband is getting angry more often and louder than you feel is reasonable, you have to be able to discuss it with him. If you can't, there's a bigger issue in your marriage than his anger. A wife must be realistic here. While it is never permissible or acceptable for anyone to get angry or to yell — after all, getting angry is forbidden — we must acknowledge the fact that it's going to happen. Sometimes it will be you and sometimes it will be him. It has to be kept in the proper perspective.

One last word on the subject. Nowadays, the expression "verbal abuse" is bantered around quite a bit. What it refers to and when one has crossed that line is not clear — after all, the expression did not originate at Har Sinai. I would, however, suggest a line. If your husband is angry and even raises his voice yet he sticks to the issue that got him upset, I wouldn't call that verbal abuse — I'd call that marriage. This may even include such expressions as "You're always doing . . ." or "You're so careless with . . ." Under the circumstances, there is something you may or may not have done that has caused his outburst. On the other hand, if he resorts to name-calling, then he has crossed a line and must be told — at a later time — that you find that sort of thing absolutely unacceptable.

CHAPTER 4

Appearance

So many sources and statements in *Chazal* deal with the idea that a woman should look pleasing to her husband. Without going into a discussion of a man's nature, suffice it to say that most men are in better moods when their wives looks good and put together. Aside from the aspect of appearance, being put together communicates the idea that your husband and his needs are important to you. That being the case, you should do your maximum in this area and try your best, within reason, to keep yourself looking your best at all times.

Although this has always been an important focus for women, it is especially vital in the current day and age, when there are so many human and technological distractions that are there for the purpose of gaining the attention of males. You don't want your husband to be able to fall back on the excuse that his wife's lack of care in this area is why he gives in to various visual temptations.

The Gemara tells a story regarding Abba Chilkiyah, who was on such a high level that he was the one to whom the other Sages came when there was a draught because it was his *tefillah* (prayer) that had the potency to change the situation. Now, please think about and internalize the following. The Gemara reports that when he would come in from his day out of the home, his wife would greet him dressed up in a beautiful manner. When asked about it by the other Sages, he explained that she did so in order that he should not look at other women. Can you imagine? We're talking about the *Gadol hador* (great man of the generation), the man with the most potent *tefillah*. Yet, even he did not deny the nature of men, and his wife acted accordingly.

Your husband is probably a wonderful person who is on a high level, but with all due respect, he is not Abba Chilkiyah. And even if he was, this is how you should relate to the fact that he is a male.

HaRav Moshe Feinstein was asked (*Even HaEzer* 1:59) about the following situation. A young lady who came from a Chassidic community where the *minhag* (custom) was for the ladies to shave their heads after marriage married a young man who was from a Chassidic community that did not have that custom. She wanted very much to follow her family's custom, but her husband objected. After discussing the ins and outs of the weight and importance of *minhagim*, Rav Moshe said it was *forbidden* for her to shave her head because she was *obligated* to carry out her husband's will in an area that he cared about. He then went on to emphasize that in no way did this cast the husband in a negative light or show that he was not on a high spiritual level for not wanting to abide by a stringency in this area. To the contrary. In his responsum, Rav Moshe cites the abovementioned Gemara about Abba Chilkiyah and says the husband is to be praised for wanting his wife's help in safeguarding himself in this matter.

One of the areas in which the concept of a wife's appearance can create strife is with regard to makeup and cosmetics. There are husbands who feel their wives look better to them without a lot, or certain types, of makeup. If that's the case, you should act in accordance with his wishes. Then there are those ladies who feel certain types of makeup are uncomfortable for them and find it annoying to apply them, whereas their husbands prefer that they do. Again, you as the wife should do as he requests. There are yet other ladies who feel that makeup and cosmetics are not within the bounds of *tznius* (modesty) that they wish to maintain. If this is the case, you must keep in mind that doing what you can to please your husband is mandatory, so a *Posek* (Halachic authority) should be asked whether you are making an accurate assessment of the situation, because if you aren't, there is no room to abide by a *chumrah* (stringency) at your husband's expense. Of course, if he wants you to apply makeup or dress in a way that crosses halachic limitations, you aren't allowed to do so, but again, you must be sure about this. It's a tricky area and probably best for you not to make this determination on your own.

The same thing goes for clothing. You should dress to please your husband, and your choice of clothes should be with him in mind. Not your neighbors, friends, or sister-in-law. Your *husband*. If you aren't sure what pleases him, ask him. If you see that he isn't happy with a certain outfit, don't wear it. It's as simple as that. The fact that you received the outfit as a gift from a close friend or it's a family heirloom worn by a *bubby* (grandmother) is wonderful. The fact that it bothers your husband is *not*. So again, please don't wear it. Maybe just save it for your own granddaughter.

This extends to head coverings as well. There are many different styles of *sheitels* (wigs) and hats. It's a good idea before investing in any of these costly items that you check with your husband to find out what he likes and, perhaps more importantly, what he *doesn't* like.

In the morning, when things are somewhat hectic and rushed, it's unreasonable to expect you to be at your best. However, in the evening, when your husband comes home, you, the wise wife, should see it as a priority to take a few minutes to put yourself together. It's inexcusable — unless it's the week before Pesach — to have your husband come home and see you looking like you were just blown out of a vacuum cleaner. Once in a while, on a particularly hectic day, it's understandable, but not on regular basis. There are times when it may not be appropriate to dress up for your husband, but at all times, you should look respectable and put together.

Sometimes, due to a busy day, there may be a conflict. You only have enough time to either put the house together before he arrives home or to put yourself together, but not both. Which one should you choose? The answer is simple. Ask *him* which *he* prefers, and then act accordingly.

Just imagine there's a knock at your door. You open it and find your mother-in-law standing there — and you look like a wreck. You know as well as I do that you'd feel devastated. With advance warning of her intended visit, you'd be sure to have the home and yourself looking like a museum, with yourself the beautiful artifact at the entrance. Your husband deserves no less; actually, he deserves much more. A queen simply doesn't allow herself to disappoint her husband due to self-neglect. So when he comes in, look your very best, in order to greet him as you would greet a king.

CHAPTER 5

Food

Food plays a major role in our lives. We eat to survive, we eat for pleasure, and we eat to celebrate. Our Shabbosim are built around food, and our Yamim Tovim (holidays) have meat and wine requirements. On a day-to-day basis, the average person eats three meals, aside from what he consumes between meals. There's no getting away from it; even people who are dieting must still eat a minimal amount each day at various intervals.

In marriage, food plays a crucial role in establishing a warm bond between husband and wife. On a regular basis, a wife prepares meals for her husband, in many cases elaborate repasts, and then her husband eats the food, praises her efforts, and thanks her. Two things have happened here: She has invested in him, which is an act of giving, and that deepens her love for him. He in turn enjoys the food, providing her with the pleasure of seeing how satisfied she's made him. He then compliments her, elaborating on each dish he's eaten, and then concludes with effusive thanks. This cycle repeats itself at least once a day at dinner, and then three times over a Shabbos.

So, clearly food is an essential relationship cementer in marriage. This is one of the reasons why providing your husband with takeout for dinner does not accomplish the same thing as when you prepare the food. Of course, there will be times and stages in life when the abovementioned preparation won't be happening on a regular basis as it does in the earlier and later stages of marriage. The needs of babies and children can be quite time-consuming if not downright overwhelming, and you just won't be able to be the culinary professional you'd like to be. However, never lose sight of the fact that a meal prepared by you for your husband accomplishes much more than just getting him fed.

If you are going into marriage with little or no cooking experience, don't be concerned. Plenty of ladies have gotten married clueless about kitchen production, yet in a short amount of time, they develop into wonderful cooks. If necessary, ask your mother or a friend for help and tips, and perhaps even spend a few days with others in their kitchens until you get the hang of it. It is a very worthwhile investment.

Obviously, you should make every effort to cook according to your husband's taste, as opposed to preparing dishes you'd like him to eat. I am not referring here to health matters, I'm referring to taste preferences. You might like to make some sort of rich cheese dish that goes by some fancy French name and thus demonstrate your culinary prowess, whereas he might prefer a simple pot roast with potatoes. Or, you'd like him to have a new chicken, broccoli, and cashew concoction which you read about in a magazine recipe section, whereas he likes simple baked chicken with a fresh salad.

The same applies — perhaps even more — to baked goods. For some reason, many women love to experiment and try new recipes for baked goods, whereas many men are happy with the old tried and tested. If brownies have been well received, don't substitute them one Shabbos with some sort of muffin thing. Chocolate chip cookies are usually preferred to some newfangled oatmeal-and-Craisins combo. In short, stick with what's been successful. If you do get that uncontrollable urge to try something creative, it's a good idea to have a sure winner in reserve just in case your new offering doesn't make it. And whatever happens, don't get upset if he doesn't enjoy it. You can't fault people for having the tastes they have. Of course, if your husband does request something new and daring, or if he is the type that will eat just about anything, then by all means ago for it.

In the early days of marriage, you should, if possible and applicable, contact your mother-in-law and find out what foods and cakes your husband enjoys. Aside from the obvious benefit of being able to please your husband right from the get-go, this will also be flattering to your mother-in-law and will help transition this tricky relationship into one of pleasant companionship. Get precise recipes and instructions for how to make those dishes, and then follow them to the letter. One word of advice: If there is a dish or cake that your mother-in-law prides herself on, and that's the one she serves when you come over, it's sometimes a good idea for you *not* to make that one at home so that she doesn't feel like there's some sort of competition. A lot depends on the type of person she is, and this must be given a bit of thought. This may become more relevant when you have children and it's in everyone's best interests that they should feel there's something special that they get only at Bubby's house.

Whatever you do, don't tamper with success. If a certain lemon cake has always been a favorite, leave well enough alone. A kugel made sweet should not be changed without advance approval, and gefilte fish made spicy should be left as is. And if you've come up with an item he loves, don't deviate. Make it the same way all the time. There's a famous saying, "The great artist knows when to stop." I always tell ladies — only partly in jest, mind you — that in many homes raisins are best left out of the kitchen. They're not good for shalom bayis. Obviously, if your husband is a raisin guy then feel free to pour them in. But if he isn't — and lots of men aren't — don't take liberties without express approval. Similarly, olives and onions, due to their strong tastes, are two of the biggest culprits. It's unwise to add them to foods or salads without being certain your husband is OK with them. In many instances, serving a dish that your husband doesn't appreciate could even be a mood changer and lead to a blowup.

Leftovers are a subject that needs to be discussed early on. Many men are fine with leftovers, whereas others really can't stand them. Contrary to the saying "They taste just like fresh," even little kids can tell the difference between freshly made food and leftovers. Foods taken out of the freezer don't magically regain their freshness.

You may be of the opinion that stuff can't be wasted, and until the leftovers get eaten you won't cook more. Before adopting this policy, check to see that your husband is on board. It's a tricky area. Your husband may prefer that there be something fresh each day and that leftovers be given to relatives or neighbors who would gladly take them. In just about all homes, it's inevitable that at least some food will get thrown out. It is indeed a shame to throw out food, but if you serve your husband leftovers and he doesn't eat them, then not only will they get thrown out anyhow, you'll also have a hungry and unhappy husband. And if he eats the leftovers under duress, he may not be hungry, but he is likely to be unhappy. Tread carefully here.

I wish to stress that even if your husband is extremely particular — some might call it picky — about his food, it is in no way an indication that he is immature or needs to work on himself in this area. Taste is very individual. You may be the type who eats basically anything, whereas he isn't. On the other hand, you may be the type who, for example, is very particular about room decor or children's clothing, and you expect to be allowed your preferences. The same applies to his food habits.

CHAPTER 6

Communication

Communication. The big *c* word. The word many feel is the number-one essential in a successful marriage. To a great extent they're right. The problem is that women and men communicate differently, and bridging this gap — maybe *chasm* is a better word — is vital for shalom bayis.

Ruby and his wife, Chani, have just finished dinner and are relaxing with cups of coffee, schmoozing about various things. After a few minutes, Chani brings up an issue that's been on her mind for a while and that's she been waiting for the right moment to talk about.

"Do you think we ought to get a new couch, Ruby?"

"Nah, I think the one we have is fine. It's a bit worn down, but it's good enough."

"Ruby, we just aren't *communicating*" Chani says in a frustrated voice.

Sound familiar?

Someone once joked that women think "communication" means agreeing with them. Whether or not it's completely true, and all joking aside, there was definitely a *miscommunication* here. It could be Ruby is simply not sensitive enough to understand his wife, and this is most likely an ongoing problem. Or it could be he is sensitive, but he thought she was genuinely asking, as opposed to saying this is something she wants, especially if she is the type that usually says straight-out what she wants. There *are* ladies like that. Whatever the case, while men have their obligations regarding how to read their wives' communication signals, there are certain things wives can do that will reduce the chances of short circuits between the two.

The first step is to speak in a way that leaves little ambiguity as to what you mean. "I would prefer we don't have guests this Shabbos" is much better than "It would be nice to have a quiet Shabbos." The first makes your position very clear. The latter leaves the option for miscommunication open and may very well end up with your husband telling you on Wednesday night that he invited a couple of yeshivah guys over. "Please call the washing machine guy tomorrow morning" is how you should express that you need an imminent repair. "It would be good if you have a chance to call the washing machine guy" communicates less urgency.

There is a manner of speaking that is referred to as trapping. For example, one person says, "Do you think it's going to rain tomorrow?"

The second person then says, "Yes."

"Oh, I disagree — I *definitely* think it *isn't*."

This sort of thing is not specific to marriage — there are people who do this habitually, and I might add, these are people who probably don't have a lot of friends. Wives do this unintentionally and certainly not in a malicious way. In the above example, Chani unintentionally set a trap for a Ruby by speaking in question form. What she wants is to hear Ruby agree to a new couch. In many cases, if the husband would respond with "What do you think?" it would be acceptable, because that would then allow the wife to say clearly what she wants. However, to some wives even that isn't good enough.

I know of one couple to whom this happened all the time. They'd go shopping, and the wife would ask the husband if he thought a certain platter she'd picked out would be good for the Shabbos table. He'd say, "What do you think?" and she would get frustrated. Or she'd ask, "Do you think we should eat out tonight?" and he'd respond, "What would you like to do?" and again she'd get upset. The irony was that he thought he was being very gracious — after all, he didn't say no — yet she was constantly becoming frustrated by his answers. It was only with rabbinic intervention that she finally understood she was — albeit unintentionally — setting a trap for him. Again, the rule is: the clearer and more direct you are — while remaining pleasant — the less chance there is for misunderstandings.

The classic area of miscommunication is when a wife kvetches or complains and the husband offers suggestions instead of empathizing. Many men are simply unaware when they first get married what is expected of them. Many others learn it but need periodic reminders that all that's needed is to listen. This has to do with the male nature and can be exasperating for a wife. Please don't let his lack of understanding get to you — it's a widespread issue. All you have to do is explain your need in a soft way, repeating it on the occasions that he forgets his role, and that's usually all that's needed.

Another important point: When a couple is sitting and schmoozing, it is not unusual to jump from one subject to another and to insert irrelevant side points. Your husband may start reminiscing about an outing you once went on, and then you mention how your aunt Leah once lost a wallet at that very location, and then you may bring up how annoying it is to lose things, and so on. Incidentally, women tend to do this far more than men. That's fine. However, this should not happen when a serious issue needs to be dealt with. So for example, if there's a burst pipe which you have to tell your husband about in the evening when he comes home, try as much as possible to stick to the point. "We have a problem that is going to need a plumber; I heard Mr. Schwartz is very reliable" should not be followed with "His son just got engaged to my friend Bella's cousin." When men deal with issues — especially money issues — there is very little else that interests them. They find trivialities exasperating when under pressure.

It goes without saying that you should make every effort not to interrupt your husband when he's speaking. You know how annoying it is to be interrupted, so you should make every attempt not to interject unrelated curiosity questions when he's telling you about an incident that took place or something of the like. The subject of women's curiosity is dealt with later in this book.

Men who are asked to do something or to take care of something that needs their attention generally do not like to be asked *when* they will be getting to it. Personally, I think a wife *should* get a specific time from her husband because men being men, the matter could easily be forgotten or put on hold for a while. However, the *way* you ask should be as pleasant as possible. "When will you do it?" may cause irritability. "I know you're really efficient — will you be able to do it by tomorrow?" is much better. The same goes for checking up on him regarding whether or not he took care of the matter.

Interestingly, there is actually a double standard here. You would take it very personally if your husband asked, "Did you remember to make kugel for Shabbos?" or "Don't forget to do the laundry today," whereas for you to ask, "Did you speak to Shlomi's rebbe (Torah teacher)?" is often a very necessary thing to do. If you have no choice but to check up on him, be sure to do it pleasantly, as discussed. "I'm so happy you said you'd talk to Shlomi's rebbe even though you're so busy. Were you able to get around to it?" is the sort of approach you should use.

There is a widespread belief, and it was probably told to you as a piece of advice before you got married by a well-meaning relative, that you and your husband should never go to sleep upset with each other. It's not true! At the end of a long day when both of you are tired and kvetchy and grumpy, an attempt to work out a small spat could turn into a major blowup accompanied by all sorts of recriminations, statements both of you will later regret having said, and eventually, tears. Far better is to recognize the fact that you're both upset, go to sleep, and then in the light of day, when things always look better than in the gloom of night, settle your differences. This is tried and tested by many. The idea of not going to sleep upset sounds good on paper, but it rarely works out in a satisfactory manner.

Ultimately, due to the differences between men and women, successful communication feeds upon itself. What this means is that as communication develops, a couple can then communicate about how they should communicate. I know this sounds funny, but it's true. Then, as their time together increases, they pick up the subtleties and nuances of what the other wants to convey, whether through tone of voice, body language, or moods.

CHAPTER 7

Privacy of Marriage

And now for the ultimate in ridiculous. The chuppah ended and the *chassan* (groom) and *kallah* (bride) entered the *yichud* room. It was the first time the couple was alone as husband and wife, the most private moment in the life of either one of them, a moment reserved for just the two of them, with no outsiders. At this most precious moment, the bride took a selfie and *posted it on her social media accounts for all to see*! I kid you not. The ultimate violation of privacy. It was a time meant to be kept between these two people — and the *entire world* got invited in! Good *grief*!!

From the moment a couple marries, they must both realize that they are now loyal to each other, and much of what goes on in their life must remain strictly between the two of them. A wife tends to have a bigger challenge with this, in part due to closeness with her mother or sister or best friend, and in part due to women being more willing to share their feelings with each other. Whatever the case, you must do all that is in your power to overcome the temptation to share information with others that is meant to remain between yourself and your husband. Many arguments and fights in marriage begin with a husband saying something like "Why did you *tell* her that?" or "You had no *business* letting your mother know!" or something along those lines. He's never right for raising his voice, but you're wrong for giving him this reason to do so. This is especially true if he has told you not to tell something to somebody specific or to anybody in general.

It may happen that your parents will ask you things about your marriage, your husband, or your husband's family. It's an awkward situation, but you must resist the temptation to give over the information. To do so is unfair to your husband. The exception to this rule is if your parents are asking about your marriage because they see you're intensely unhappy and they suspect their assistance is needed. However, nothing asked purely out of curiosity should be answered. Furthermore, reporting a flaw you've seen in your husband or mentioning something he's done wrong, besides being inherently inappropriate, will very possibly, if it somehow gets back to him, create a volcanic explosion that would put real mountains to shame. In a word, well, three, actually: don't do it!

When a husband finds out that his wife has given over information that he feels she shouldn't have, there is a sense of betrayal. This extends to money matters, child-rearing issues, future plans of any nature, or the general state of the marriage. You should live with the following rule always in mind: if you have any doubt at all as to whether or not you should be sharing certain information with anyone other than your husband, you mustn't do it unless you've cleared it with your husband first. That means express approval, not an assumption. On the other hand, sharing regular day-to-day occurrences and trivialities that you know for certain he won't object to is fine. However, don't be surprised if you tell someone something you think is harmless, for example, that your husband got a parking ticket, and then he gets upset about it. As the old saying goes, no one ever regretted *not* saying something.

There may be times when you need outside advice regarding how to deal with certain situations. In most cases, you should get your husband's OK to speak to a *Rav* or counselor. On the other hand, there are exceptional situations where a wife has no choice but to get outside assistance without her husband's knowledge or consent. An example would be a wife who feels her husband's temper is out of control and she can't even speak to him about it without him exploding. Another example would be if the husband isn't functioning due to depression or some other cause and the wife has no choice but to look for outside assistance on her own.

You and your husband may have to discuss what sort of things shouldn't be shared with outsiders. Some people are very private and others are all over the place. There's no right or wrong here, and in a well-functioning marriage this can spoken about, and some sort of understanding can be reached.

CHAPTER 8

Controlling Curiosity

Megillas Esther says that Vashti made a banquet for the ladies. The Medrash asks what they were doing at that lavish affair. It goes on to say that she gave them a guided tour of the king's palace. She said, "This is where the king eats; this is where he sleeps, etc." The Medrash then concludes with the statement, "We see from here that women want to know everything." In our terms, it means women are curious — extremely, insatiably, and almost compulsively curious.

Like all statements of *Chazal* regarding women, there is nothing deprecating or demeaning intended here. It is simply a statement of fact. This is how Hashem created women, and He did so for a very beneficial purpose. A woman's curiosity often keeps her husband and family members out of trouble.

For example, Yirmi comes home with a new briefcase, and the following conversation takes place.

"Where did you get it?" asks wife Debbie.

"Geula."

"How much did it cost?"

"A hundred forty shekels."

"Which store?"

"Beit HaTik."

"Were there any other colors?"

"Not too many."

"Were there a lot of people in the store?"

"So-so."

"What time did you go?"

A moment of silence. "Uh, about twelvish."

"But that's in the middle of *seder*, isn't it?"

So due to her curiosity, Debbie has uncovered an important piece of information. She can then discuss with Yirmi — at an appropriate time, of course — the idea of commitment to learning and sticking to *kollel* rules. If Yirmi is a working man, she could bring up the subject of stealing from one's boss by taking time off without his approval. This is a positive use of the trait.

A woman's curiosity can also be used to find out who in the neighborhood needs help after birth, who needs a *shidduch* (marriage partner), and other such mitzvah endeavors. The challenge in possessing this characteristic is that it must be controlled and suppressed when it comes to asking about people due to *lashon hara* (derogatory speech) concerns. This is of particular concern in marriage, where a husband and wife spend so much time speaking to each other, and it's only natural that the wife will want to know all the details of her husband's life, including the people that he's involved with. Extreme caution must be exercised here.

Men and women are very different in this regard. I'll show you two instances — out of many — where you can see this clearly. Any time I've given a talk or *shiur* to ladies, if a latecomer enters, almost every head in the room turns to see who arrived. If the *shiur* is for men, there are very few who do so. If the talk is interesting, they don't pay attention to someone walking in, and if it's not, a good percentage are asleep. Few turn to the door.

The second instance is the way ladies tell things to their husbands and to others. "My cousin Sheila," begins Temma, "the one whose husband is an accountant, made a *shidduch* — I think it's her fourth or fifth one. It's with Mr. Klien's son. Mr. Klien took over the appliance business from his father. I think his parents moved to Florida. His son learns at — I mean, now he's at Beis Torah, before that I'm not sure — I think at Marbei Limmud . . ." and on and on. Notice that she is consistently inserting various details. A man, on the other hand, is likely to just say "Sheila's daughter is engaged to Kleins' son."

With the above in mind, please be aware that there is something men can get very annoyed with that is a direct result of female curiosity. Let's say Zevulun starts telling his wife, Elka, about an incident that took place on the bus.

"So I get on the bus—"

"What number?"

"A fifty-nine. Anyhow, these three guys get on—"

"At which stop?"

"By the falafel shop. Listen. So one of them—"

"How old were they?"

"It doesn't matter — just listen for a second, will ya? One of them goes to the driver—"

"Was it a regular bus or an accordion bus?"

Sound familiar?

Or it could be a husband is excited about something, like that he got a promotion or a raise. He wants to tell his wife about it, and, as is the norm when people tell over things like this, he wants to express his excitement by relating how the event unfolded.

"The boss called me in—"

"Did he email you or call?"

"He called. Anyhow, I go into his office—"

"What does it look like?"

"Doesn't matter." The husband is starting to get frustrated. "So he says, 'Berel—'"

"Is he the one you told me always wears really nice ties?"

Berel eventually gets so irritated by the constant interruptions that he says, "Oh, never mind," and the two lapse into an uncomfortable silence, or in some cases, a spat.

This can also happen at the Shabbos table. Yigal finally has everyone's attention and starts his *dvar Torah* (Torah thought). "The Ohr HaChaim says—"

"My friend Miri went to his *kever* (grave) last week," interrupts wife Bella.

"Uh-huh. Anyhow, he says that Moshe Rabbeinu—"

"Wow, I forgot to tell you my second cousin Moshe Weiss got his *semichah* (Rabbinical ordination)!"

This sort of thing could easily result in a husband clamming up and the rest of what could have been a wonderful *seudah* (meal) turning into a tense affair.

The bottom line is that you have to work on this. It's not easy since it's part of your inherent makeup. It's perfectly normal that you'll be burning with curiosity as to various insignificant details of whatever it is your husband will be telling you about. However, you must suppress the urge to interrupt. If you consciously work on it, you'll improve. You won't likely be perfect — after all, it's your nature — but you'll get better as time goes on. Your husband may have to give you a reminder once in a while to please not ask him questions in the middle, and you should tell him to let you know if you've lapsed back into constant interrupting. And if you do catch yourself doing it, you should say, "Oh, sorry about that. I'm trying; I really am." You can also point out once in a while to your husband that you feel there has definitely been an improvement in this area and that you'd like to hear from him that he's noticed it.

Just don't interrupt him when he explains how he's noticed it.

CHAPTER 9

Independent Decisions

It's Thursday morning. Sima and Zelig are discussing their plans for the upcoming Shabbos.

"I'd really like to stay home and have a quiet Shabbos," Zelig says. "It's been a tough week and I'm exhausted. I really don't have the energy for socializing."

"No problem," Sima answers. "I'd also like to just have a relaxing bit of time together."

Late Thursday night, Zelig is enjoying a piece of potato kugel and reading the paper.

"Oh, I forgot to tell you," Sima says. "Mrs. Kirsch invited us for the Friday-night meal, so I told her we'll come."

"But we decided we were staying home," protests Zelig.

"I know. But I figured you wouldn't mind because they're such nice people, and besides, once she invited us I couldn't say no."

"You certainly could have," a suddenly angry Zelig snaps. "You should've just told her it won't work out this week. Who's more *important* — me or *her*?!"

"Oh, don't make such a big deal out of it," Sima says defensively. "It's only a short walk and a *seudah*."

"Don't tell me not to make a big *deal*," Zelig barks. "It *is* a big deal! We made a decision together and you have no right to change it without telling me. You're always *doing* stuff like that and I don't *like* it!"

The argument escalates, accusations fly back and forth, and a harmonious marriage has turned into a battleground. If Sima had thought it was uncomfortable to turn down the invitation, it'll be even *more* uncomfortable when Zelig says he's not going and that she should pick up the phone to cancel.

How could this have been avoided?

Without getting into how wrong it is for Zelig to raise his voice — that's dealt with in the men's book — Sima must realize that she broke a rule here and that any fallout is to a large degree her fault. It is an immutable principle in marriage that when a decision has been reached jointly, neither the husband nor the wife is allowed to change the decision without discussing it again with their spouse. There are rare exceptions, but they are few and far between. You and your husband are functioning as a team, and you must always abide by the rules of teamwork. When you veer off of a mutual decision, it is both unfair and, to a certain extent, a lack of loyalty to your husband. Few things infuriate husbands as much as this.

The argument that you have been placed in an uncomfortable position, as in the invitation example above, is not valid. Internalizing the fact that your first priority is your husband will help you negotiate even those tricky and uncomfortable situations. "I have to speak to my husband" is a very important phrase that should always be at the forefront of your consciousness. This could come up with regard to purchases, invitations, suggestions, and many other situations that can arise. It will allow you a time buffer so that you don't have to make an on-the-spot decision, will show loyalty to your husband, and in many cases, will allow him to present a perspective you might not have thought of. An additional side benefit is that it will take a lot of pressure off you because anyone hearing you say so will realize that it's a perfectly reasonable things to do (and that they themselves should probably be doing it). So repeat after me: "I have to speak to my husband. I have to speak to my husband. I have to . . ."

Of course, the area where this can really trigger explosions is finances. Sima and Zelig patched up the Shabbos fiasco, and are now (probably a good few days later) discussing buying a new couch. They come to a decision that the old one will do for the time being and down the line they'll see what's doing. Money is a bit tight right now. They could push it if they really have to, but another half a year won't hurt.

Two days later, Sima informs Zelig that she changed her mind and ordered the couch after all. Zelig explodes.

"You *what*?! How could you do that?! We decided *not* to get it right now. This means now I'll have to scramble to get the credit card covered and then figure out how to get next month's budget taken care of!" He goes on and on about how wrong it was for her to make an independent decision and what upheaval it's going to cause to their finances.

Aside from raising his voice and getting angry, he's well within his rights to protest. Sima should have had the decency to bring the topic up again and see if she and Zelig could reach a different decision.

Please understand, I don't mean in any way that the husband should have all the say. Sima has every right to be involved in decision-making, and in most cases I urge men to give in to their wives' wishes. The issue here is Sima making an *independent* decision *after a joint one had been reached*.

This includes situations where the wife feels she wasn't really happy with the original decision and only agreed to it under duress. If that's the case, the couple has to work out a method for resolving differences. But under no circumstances should she simply bypass her husband.

CHAPTER 10

Realistic Expectations

It's Friday morning. Label and Bruchi are going to the Feldmans for the Shabbos-day *seudah*.

"Label, when you're in town, could you pick up a gift and drop it off by the Feldmans'? We won't be able to give it to them on Shabbos," Bruchi says on Friday morning.

"Sure, no problem," Label answers happily.

I'm so fortunate to have such a cooperative husband! Bruchi thinks to herself.

A few hours later, Label comes home with the groceries Bruchi had asked him to pick up. He forgot the tomatoes and bought kohlrabi instead of cabbage, but other than that he got everything on the list.

"Did you drop something off at the Feldmans'?" Bruchi asks.

"I sure did!" Label answers proudly.

"What did you get?"

"Well, I figured flowers are a bit trite, and wine is so common, and candy . . ."

"Label, what did you *get*?"

A big smile forms across Label's face, from ear to ear. "You know, Benny Feldman is really good with his hands, so I bought them a really good wrench."

"You *didn't* — tell me you didn't!" Bruchi says in disbelief.

"I sure did. Who would expect . . ."

"*Labellllllll*! Are you *serious*?! A *wrench*?! *Nobody* buys a *wrench* as a Shabbos gift! A *wrench*?! *Labelllll*! *What were you thinking*?!"

While this example is, hopefully, a bit extreme, similar occurrences can and do happen in many, if not most, marriages, much to the consternation of the wife, who, besides wishing for a wrench to use on her husband, wonders how a man could be so *utterly* clueless. So please allow me to shed a bit of light on this situation.

You got married with a certain image of what your husband would be like. He would fulfill all the dreams you had as a little girl when you drifted off to fantasy land regarding what your *chassan* would be like. He'd listen attentively when you'd speak, he'd always clean up after himself, he'd anticipate your needs from *a* to *z*, and in general he'd make you happy, fulfilled, and content 24/7. This is the attitude that's been imbibed through exposure to fairy tales that end with "And they lived happily ever after" and all sorts of Hollywood brainwashing.

Then, after a short period of marriage, you realize things are not going to be the way you imagined. In many cases, not even close. He leaves his clothes on the floor, makes suggestions when all you need is a listening ear, doesn't pick up a broom when he sees the room needs to be swept, and certainly comes up way short when it comes to anticipating your preferences. While much of the problem is due to a lot of young guys really not being aware of what marriage will entail, part of the problem is that you got married with somewhat unrealistic expectations.

The first area where expectations must be reduced is that of your husband anticipating your needs and the needs of the home. Believe it or not, a man may very well be unaware that he shouldn't make suggestions when his wife is kvetching. This is something so basic yet so commonly a cause of female frustration. You had in mind that any time you needed empathy he'd be sensitive to it. The reality is that while there are certainly some men who understand this instinctively, there are lots who don't. A *frum* (religious) male has spent the vast majority of his life around other males, and empathy is just not a big thing there; suggestions and corrections are the name of the game. Sure, he was told in *chassan* classes that this is what's expected, but by the time the chuppah rolled around it's likely he had long forgotten.

The solution? Explain to him, nicely, that what's needed under the circumstances is to simply listen and be empathetic. It's not something you expected that you would have to do, but not to do so will only leave you more frustrated.

The same goes for household cleanup. A young husband may be under the impression that his wife will be taking care of domestics and that he isn't expected to participate. It is not unlikely that he was raised by a mother who basically did everything and all he did was throw a blanket over his bed every morning — the male idea of making a bed — or vacuum once in a while on *erev Shabbos* (the eve of Shabbos; Friday) if his mother asked him to do it and then reminded him about it several times. Or it could be that he isn't bothered by clutter and mess and doesn't realize that others, in this case you, are. You'll have to clue him in and let him know how you'd like the home to look and that if he ever sees it not looking that way, he should feel free to lend a hand without being told. Then, if he ever does lend a hand, be happy, but don't expect a onetime discussion to result in remarkable consistency on his part.

Some wives expect their husbands to pick up household goods without being told. In many cases this is a mistake. Lots of men wait to hear from their wives what needs to be bought. The thinking — or lack thereof — that lies behind this is that the wife does the cooking and feeding, so she knows better what's needed in the house.

Then there are those men who actually do take the initiative but buy the wrong things. They don't know that their wife doesn't use a certain detergent — cheap as it is — or that another box of Cheerios isn't needed because there is a healthy supply in the pantry. Again, the solution is to drop the expectations and makes things perfectly clear.

Some wives have had to tell their husbands that on an anniversary or birthday they would like to receive a gift.

Please understand, a man may have been raised in a home where no one made a big deal out of birthdays, which is more common than you think, or an anniversary was celebrated with a trip to a restaurant.

The first time it happens that you aren't on the receiving end when you expect to be will be disappointing, but with effective communication of your needs it will be the last time. There are even extreme cases where a husband has to be told by his wife that she would appreciate hearing compliments. Perhaps he didn't hear his father praise his mother very often. Alternatively, even when there are compliments, they may not be frequent enough to satisfy you, in which case you must explain to him what you'd like in this regard. Most extreme of all, there are men who may not realize that after they eat a meal they should thank their wife and praise her efforts. It's rare, but not unheard of. In the unlikely event that it applies to you, a bit of educating is called for.

While you may feel a bit saddened that the knight in shining armor of your dreams never quite materialized, clarifying your needs will go a long way toward bringing him nearer to that point. It's certainly better than having your husband drop off a wrench as a Shabbos gift.

Another area that can potentially be a source of stress and tension is with regard to babies and small children. A husband may hear a baby crying yet doesn't move a muscle in his direction. His wife is thinking, *Doesn't he* hear *the baby? What, is he only* my *child? Isn't he the father?* A very common scenario: The couple has guests at the Shabbos table and the baby starts screaming in his crib. Each spouse is waiting for the other to get up from the table and deal with the child. Or it can be a diaper that is long overdue for a change which the husband seems to think will get taken care of on its own, meaning, by anyone but him. Again, the best approach is to talk things over and reach a point of clarity as far as what expectations you have of your husband. Please keep in mind, as I've mentioned elsewhere in this book, that all these discussions and clarifications should be done pleasantly and at the right time.

The bottom line is: in all areas, don't expect perfection, but with good communication you can anticipate improvement.

CHAPTER 11

Erev Shabbos and Yom Tov

Let's face the facts. In most homes, there is more stress than usual on *erev Shabbos* and *erev Yom Tov*. It might not be overt and it might not lead to a row, but it isn't far beneath the surface, and on these days, it usually takes less than usual to set off some fireworks.

The wife feels the pressure to create a beautiful Shabbos week after week for her family, and regardless of how much help she gets, the brunt of the responsibility falls squarely on her shoulders. Cooking, baking, cleaning, making sure the clothes are washed and pressed — at the end of the day it's all on her. This is especially the case when there are guest coming for some or all of the meals. If there are little kids underfoot it's even tougher. She may also be either expecting or nursing, which makes matters that much harder. If she expects or has asked for help and isn't getting it, the potential for unpleasantness increases.

This volatile atmosphere is so common that in various sources and *sefarim* we are told to be cautious not to allow the shalom in the home to be ruined on *erev Shabbos*. Of course, when a husband sees his wife stressed, he regularly shares nuggets of wisdom, such as "You've always made it on time, so you will this week too" or "If you wouldn't bake there wouldn't be so much pressure" or "Do the ironing earlier in the week and that will give you more time" — and we all know these do absolutely nothing for the wife's state of mind. Well, maybe not nothing — they get her *more* irritated than she already was. I myself on many occasions have played the role of *erev Shabbos* coach, but somehow my team has always lost.

In some cases, the tension and pressure could be quite extreme. Consider the following true incident. A young man, we'll call him Moshe, arrived at Ohr Somayach. He told me he came from a *frum* home but was not really interested in *Yiddishkeit* (Judaism).

"I do keep Shabbos, but I really *hate* it," he told me.

"Because of all the restrictions?" I asked, assuming that was the issue. No phone, no car, no computer — the usual.

"No, I don't mind not doing stuff. I just hate the whole Shabbos thing."

"Why? Didn't your mom make a lot of good food?"

"Oh, she did — *lots* of food. And sitting at the table with my Dad wasn't so bad. But on *erev Shabbos*, my mother was *such* a nervous wreck. She spent the whole day yelling and screaming at us. I couldn't stand it. I'd rather eat a salami sandwich than have to go through all that."

This is how bad it could be.

So what's the solution? To expect no tension is unrealistic, but with a bit of work on oneself, coupled with an understanding of men, a lot of the stress and unpleasantness could be avoided. The first step is to realize that when it comes to domestics, men are often unreliable and can easily be distracted. What you should do is explain in advance, in a pleasant way, the type of help you need and what you expect your husband to do. Really spell it out clearly, and make a written list, which you should then place somewhere he'll be sure to constantly see it. This should be done well before *erev Shabbos*. I suggest you prepare a delicious supper on a Tuesday night or go out to a restaurant. Whichever it is, pick a time and setting in which you are both relaxed, with no background noise or distractions, and then clarify how you'd like *erev Shabbos* to work.

If it's the shopping you want him to do, don't leave anything to chance. Men have a knack for picking up everything except the one thing you need the most. Make a list and emphasize to him that he should get absolutely everything on it. He should make no independent decision that any given item is not really needed.

If you want his help with the cleaning, tell him clearly what needs to be done and provide him with the cleaning products and rags you want him to use. Many men are more than happy to help out, but they don't know, through no fault of their own, where you keep stuff, and even if they do know, you probably have certain cleaning products and brushes that you do or don't want them to use. Taking care of this in advance is a lot better than having him yell to ask you from the back room where the floor cleaner is while you have your head in a hot oven checking to see if the chicken is done.

Most of us have heard at some point from our mothers, "If you're going to do it, do it with a smile." You may be tempted to say this to your husband, who pulls a face when you ask him for some form of help on *erev Shabbos* — or at any other time, for that matter. Don't. For one thing, I don't think you always do everything with a smile. There are plenty of tasks that are not enjoyable, but they have to get done, smile or not. I don't think most ladies are happy as a lark when they scrub crusty cholent pots on *motza'ei Shabbos*, right? Your husband may grumble a bit about being asked to do something, especially after he already did something else and he thought he was done for the day. It's inadvisable to make an issue out of it as it can lead to a blowup, with him saying, "I already did so much around here, etc." Just let it go. Perhaps at a different time when you're both relaxed, you can bring up that you'd really like it if he could drop the grumbling, but think carefully about whether or not there's really a chance of it happening, and then proceed accordingly.

CHAPTER 12

Husband Versus Kids

Bachurim for the most part are basically clueless regarding what marriage really entails. They usually see it as something that will provide companionship and will allow for their needs to be taken care of. They've heard that they will have to do a lot of giving, but many simply don't realize what it can and will entail. Those with more mature thinking realize there will be challenges and that they'll be expected to put someone else's needs ahead of their own, but in most cases, reality will still exceed anything they imagined. *Bachurettes* tend to be more realistic and have a more natural insight into what it's really all about.

A *bachur* goes through a development process. First he spends time learning how to deal with someone who is so different from himself in so many ways. He needs a minimum of nine months to internalize this. During this time he may get a crash course in how to deal with that someone when she's expecting. When the first baby makes his or her appearance, and then when more children come along, especially in fast succession, he realizes he has to grow up. I mean, to really and truly grow up. This section will deal with how you can help him make this transition while maintaining shalom bayis. It's not easy.

When expecting, which can be accompanied by various discomforts, coupled with utter exhaustion, it's a good idea for you to sit down with your husband early on and explain what is happening and what can be expected. Again, most young married guys haven't got the faintest idea of what pregnancy entails and how extreme things can get. They've heard about morning sickness and pickle cravings, but that's about it. Spell things out for him, assuming he knows nothing, and apologize in advance — even though you certainly can't be faulted — for the times when you won't be the cheery, upbeat, and energetic girl that he married. Let him know you will probably be sleeping more, and you may not be able to make the kind of meals he likes, either due to a lack of energy or an inability to be around certain foods and smells. It is also advisable to mention those things that you've been able to do up until now but that under the circumstances will require either help from him or him taking over completely.

The same applies when a baby is born. Let your husband know what your limitations will be during the period of recuperation from the birth and what duties he will have regarding care of the child in general. Again, mention should be made of the fact that meals will not be as elaborate as in the past and sometimes won't be made at all. An important piece of advice is to keep the fridge well stocked with cold cuts and other quick edibles. No joke. Also explain to him that he will be expected to get up in the middle of eating to care for a screaming baby.

The more these things are clarified in advance, the less stress there will be on the shalom bayis. Notice, I didn't say there won't be *any* stress. Babies and children can and do present many challenges to marital harmony. A mature and focused couple must work hard and work together in order to maintain peace in the home once they become parents.

At some stage in the early days of childbearing and child-rearing, most women get to a point where they are falling off their feet. This can be the result of, among other things, constant nursing, a colicky baby, or extreme lack of sleep. This is where the test of *middos* comes in. As the Vilna Gaon says, the reason we were put into this world is to rectify our *middos*. Perhaps at no time are *middos* tested as much as when an overtired couple are up in the middle of the night — yet again — with one baby or more. Just about anything that either one says can trigger an unpleasant response and lead to a big fight. Therefore, you must discuss in advance how you will be dealing with this type of situation, including who will be on duty and during what times. The wisest thing to do in the middle of the night is to be as silent as possible. The less talking, the better. If you both happen to be in wonderful moods at two a.m. after three straight nights of lack of sleep, this book is probably something *you* should have written.

As the kids get older, you will have more time to devote to your husband. Obviously, when there is a conflict between your husband's needs and the needs of the children, as long as the children can't fend for themselves you'll have to take care of them. However, when the children get a bit older, there will be times when you could put energy into your husband without it compromising the care of your children. This is where your responsibility as a wife can be tested. If a man feels that somehow he isn't on the receiving end due to his wife's focus on the children when she really doesn't have to be focused on them, that can cause fallout in the marriage. It can be tricky knowing where to draw the line, but Hashem gave you the tools to do so, in keeping with the verse "*Chachmos noshim bonsoh beisah*, The wisest of women build their home" (*Mishlei* 14:1).

CHAPTER 13

Timing

In married life, there are a lot of issues that come up. Some are fairly trivial, some are important, and some are urgent. One source of strife in the home is issues being brought up at inopportune moments. Correct timing can spell the difference between a home full of tension and a home functioning with tranquility. Timing is everything.

A wise man once said: When your husband comes home at night, two important things have to happen: he needs to eat, and you need to tell him how hard your day was. If done in the proper order, the home will be like Gan Eden. If done out of order, well, you can fill in the end of the sentence.

Let's take an example. Shmuli walks in at the end of the day. As he's putting his hat and jacket away, he says, "How was your day, Ruchi?"

"Oh it was so *frustrating*. Simcha's rebbe called and said he's not doing as well as he could be—"

"I *told* you he needs extra tutoring," Shmuli cuts in unkindly.

"Yeah, but besides that, I had to pick up the groceries and there was no parking space—"

"Why didn't you go on Tuesday night like I told you?" Shmuli snaps.

"You think it's so *easy* to get out of the house?" Ruchi snaps back. "But besides that, the washing machine guy came and said we have to get ready for a new machine because this one's on the way out."

"Those guys *always* say that. There's nothing *wrong* with our machine!"

They then sit down to a tense and unhappy dinner, and the evening only gets worse from there.

Now, in most cases, all this could have been avoided. Ruchi should have greeted Shmuli with a smile, and she should have gotten him to the dinner table as soon as possible. Then, after he was no longer irritable from hunger, and after unloading her frustrations that simply needed a bit of listening from an attentive husband, and a bit of chatting, she could have asked him to sit down with some cake and a drink and go through the various issues that must be dealt with more seriously. It's all about the timing.

The same thing goes for sharing unpleasant news. Before anything, a wise wife must decide if a certain piece of news is something her husband really needs to hear about. Not all bad news has to be told. I know of a family that has a policy that bad news is not given over unless family members need to know about it because they will be participating in a *levayah* (funeral) or being *menachem avel* (comforting a mourner). Any other bad news is left for all family members to find out through other means, and if they never hear about it, nothing has been lost.

If and when, *chas v'shalom* (God forbid), such news does need to be given over, or anything else distressing must be discussed, it's only fair to allow your husband to eat dinner calmly and then, some time later, to break the news to him. This requires a great deal of self-control, but you'd be surprised at what you're capable of if you feel something is important enough. Blurting out the bad tidings as soon as your husband walks into the house is not appropriate.

The Medrash says that Rebbe Meir's two sons died on *leil Shabbos* (Friday night). His wife covered the bodies and kept the news from Rebbe Meir the entire Shabbos, only informing him once Shabbos ended. Imagine the kind of restraint and self-control that required. Aside from whatever other lessons this Medrash teaches us, I have little doubt it also comes to demonstrate what kind of restraint a wife is capable of if she cares enough about her husband.

A certain *Rosh Yeshivah* (dean of a yeshivah) and his wife did not have children for quite a few years. After doing various tests, they went to the specialist who had been dealing with their case to get results. The husband stayed in the waiting room while his wife went in to the professor.

"I'm sorry to tell you this," the professor said, "but based on the test results, you are never going to have children."

A few minutes later, the wife went out and her husband asked anxiously, "What did the professor say?"

"He said everything will be fine," she answered with a relaxed smile.

Could you imagine what that took? She didn't want to aggravate her husband in spite of the obviously intense pain and distress she was feeling just then. Unbelievable. We're not talking here about the wife of a Tanna — this is a woman who lived a short time ago. Again, we see what a wife is capable of if something is important enough to her.

Oh, yeah, I forgot to mention — the couple ended up having nine kids. I'm certainly not sure, but who knows if it wasn't in the merit of her sensitivity to her husband?

There may be times when you have to criticize your husband or point out a flaw that he needs to fix. Be sure to only do this when both of you are in good moods. If you aren't, it will come off as you picking on him and he won't be responsive to it in the way you hoped. And if he isn't in a good mood, it'll only make his mood worse.

Furthermore, you should never correct him in front of others. Almost anything he did or said that you feel was inappropriate can be related to him privately afterwards. This applies to the Shabbos table as well, where he may have given over incorrect information about the *parashah*, or he dominated the conversation. Men are very sensitive to being corrected in general, and when done in front of others, it's a recipe for disaster.

In the course of time, you'll learn from experience what to say and when to say it. Perhaps even more importantly, you'll learn when *not* to say, though I think it won't take nearly as long to figure that one out.

CHAPTER 14

Punctuality

One of the glaring differences between men and women is the way they relate to time. *Frum* men are very time focused. There are davening times and *sedarim* (learning sessions) and all sorts of schedule-related matters. While women do have time-related demands, such as driving car pool or getting supper ready, especially women who work out of the home, as a rule they are less attuned to the passage of time. This is why countless comic skits have used this difference as a theme, creating all sorts of situations where a woman's lateness leads to supposedly funny results.

While husbands must take this difference into account and not hold their wives to the same standard as themselves, there are a few things a wife could do in order to avoid punctuality-related conflict.

Let's say a couple made up to meet for dinner or to go shopping at a certain time. If the wife is delayed due to responsibilities in the home, such as a baby who won't calm down or some other problem, she certainly can't be faulted. By the time she got all the kids organized and dinner made, she was running late. It happens quite often. She should certainly call her husband as soon as she realizes she will be delayed, but more than that can't be expected. In the days before cell phones — believe it or not, there was such a time — it was often not possible to contact one's husband. Then, men really had to work on their *middos* when kept waiting.

However, there are optional things that a wife may get involved in, such as schmoozing with a friend or finishing up something in the home that could certainly be done later, like decorating a cake. In such cases, it is inconsiderate on her part to keep her husband waiting. It communicates the idea that he just isn't as important to her as he should be. Not only is it not good for shalom bayis, it's not good for her personally, as it reinforces the feeling she may have that her husband can be taken for granted.

In the event that it does happen, please be sure to apologize and mention that it was really not proper. Sometimes women forget to do that. A wife may think, *I do so much for him; he should just cut me some slack*, or worse yet, she might say it to her irritated husband. Such an attitude is unacceptable. It's particularly important to think about the fact that if this had been anyone else, you'd probably apologize profusely. Well, your husband deserves no less consideration than anyone else — actually, he deserves more.

It may also happen that the couple is supposed to leave the house together to go to a wedding or somewhere else, and at the time they had agreed upon to leave the wife is still at the height of her preparations. The husband must keep in mind that it takes ladies a lot longer to get ready than men. Men generally need to change a tie or a belt and that's it, whereas for women going out is an entire project.

However, the wife should take into account the amount of time she'll need and begin sooner if necessary and possible.

There is also the issue of long goodbyes. For some reason, women who have already said goodbye to each other can and do then stand at the door still talking, and it could go on for a while. Men find this extremely irritating and inconsiderate, as they are usually already outside and just standing and waiting while time passes. This causes so many needless quarrels and could actually produce a sour end to what would have otherwise been a very enjoyable evening. What I recommend is that the ladies begin saying goodbye about fifteen minutes before the time they've made up to meet or leave with their husbands, and then everyone can go home happy.

One situation that can be a source of tension is when davening ends. A wife may be standing outside shul schmoozing with countless friends while her husband, who happens to be hungry and would like to get home for the *seudah*, just stands there waiting. Men usually try to be understanding and patient, but at a certain point it becomes more than they can take. They get irritated, and then the pleasant Shabbos mood is ruined.

In most marriages this time-related business isn't a major shalom bayis issue, but it does come up from time to time and must be dealt with properly.

CHAPTER 15

Appreciating Him

Everyone knows how important it is to feel and show appreciation when others have done something for us, what is called in Hebrew *hakaras hatov*. There is no one in the world to whom a wife should feel and show *hakaras hatov* more than her husband. He keeps her company, brings *ruchniyus* into her home, and provides a listening ear, encouragement, and a slew of other things.

I would have placed "provides for her" at the top of the list, but in today's world, in which so many men are learning full-time and the wives are the breadwinners, I could envision those female heads shaking and saying, "This Kapan guy is *so* wrong." However, at a minimum, we can say he has taken on the *commitment* to provide for her, which means that if at any point and for any reason a wife stops working, the husband has a halachic obligation to take care of the financial needs of the family.

Whatever the case, if you think about it you'll see that in spite of his imperfections and flaws and all the times he forgets an item on the shopping list and all the times he left and will leave his socks on the floor and all the times he did not speak in that sweet, loving tone of voice, at the end of the day you should still feel a tremendous sense of gratitude toward him.

If you're still not convinced, try to tap into the way you felt and your emotional state before meeting him for the first time, when you wanted *so much* to get married and it hadn't yet happened. A tissue, anyone?

The Gemara says one shouldn't throw a stone into a well he drank out of. The idea is that one has a debt of gratitude to the well, so to throw a stone in would be a sign of being an ingrate. The obvious question asked by many is, since a well is an inanimate object, who cares if you throw a stone in or not? The answer is that doing so would cause a person to lose some degree of their *hakaras hatov* sensitivity.

Now, your husband is not an inanimate object. I know that at times it seems so, like on Shabbos after he's had a few helpings of cholent or at two a.m. when the baby is screaming and hubby maintains his log-like condition, but the reality is that he isn't inanimate. As such, regardless of his shortcomings, you should feel and practice *hakaras hatov* towards him.

The nature of marriage is such that it's easy to take your spouse for granted, especially when he's been on a streak of messing up, which happens periodically. It's advisable, therefore, to constantly make an effort to remind yourself how very much you owe him and to take concrete steps to demonstrate your appreciation. This applies also — perhaps especially — to those things that he has an *obligation* to do or to take care of.

I once read about a couple that had shalom bayis trouble. At some point, the *Rav* working with them asked the husband where he felt the problem lay.

"My wife never thanks me for anything I do," the husband answered.

"Is that true?" the *Rav* asked the wife.

"Yes."

"Why don't you thank him?"

"It's his job to do those things. Why should I thank him?"

True, he has obligations. Then again, a wife is obligated, for example, to cook for her husband. Doesn't every wife expect and deserve thanks for the meal she prepared?

This doesn't end with wives and husbands either. A bus driver should be thanked even though it's his job to drive a bus, as should an accountant, doctor, electrician, store owner, and anyone else who provides a service, in spite of the fact that they are being paid for what they do or that it is their job. This is basic decency.

Wives do sometimes overlook this. They may thank their husbands for doing something out of the ordinary, like driving their aunt to the airport or running an errand they really have no connection to. But something like mopping the floor or doing the dishes or playing with the kids may get taken for granted. So please remember, just as you expect to be thanked for doing laundry or shopping or paying the bills, he has the same expectations.

In keeping with the principle that external actions affect our inner feelings and moods, doing something like baking his favorite pie out of the clear blue on a Tuesday evening and attaching a note saying, "Thank you for being you," or something mushy like that, will not only convey to him how you feel, it will reinforce those feelings within yourself. Additionally, it's a good idea once in a while to sit down for a half hour or so and make a list of all the ways in which he has enriched your life. You can keep the list in a place where you can look it over when things aren't as smooth as you wish they would be. You can add to the list as new benefits occur to you. Mind you, this is all for your own benefit. And if you become especially ambitious, you can present the list to him, accompanied, of course, by a dinner featuring his favorite cut of beef. This sort of thing has many side benefits.

Please keep in mind that I am not referring here to the concept of encouragement discussed earlier in the book. Encouragement and appreciation are two separate concepts.

One of the things that can sidetrack a wife from this sense of gratitude is looking at other women and comparing her husband to theirs. One man is a bigger *masmid* (diligent in his Torah learning), one earns more money, one seems to be more of a gentleman, one is more charismatic, and so on and so forth. While no wife with any degree of common sense would ever bring it up verbally to her husband, there are those who do focus on it in the privacy of their minds, or worse yet, in conversation with their mothers, sisters, or friends. This focus, which is really not fair because you married him for who he is, has the additional negative effect of causing you to lose a sense of appreciation for him.

Now that you're done reading this chapter, maybe sit down and type up that list. It'll go well with a freshly baked cherry pie.

CHAPTER 16

Ten Minutes a Day

In the men's volume I wrote that the single most important piece of advice in the book is that a man should find ten minutes a day to read a book on shalom bayis. The idea is that not treating one's wife as one should stems for the most part from taking one's focus off the importance of marriage. This is not an original idea of mine; this concept appears in the introduction to the *Mesillas Yesharim*, where the Ramchal writes that the reason we demonstrate improper *middos* despite knowing how wrong that is is due to taking our focus off the importance of working on our *middos*. A daily dose of reminder does wonders for marriage.

To a certain extent, but to a much lesser degree, the advice applies to ladies as well. A woman's nature, combined with the role she plays as primary homemaker, keeps her pretty much focused on her marriage — far more than a man, who, due to being out of the home more, can easily become sidetracked. On the other hand, there is always the possibility of taking one's husband for granted, so to counter that, it is advisable for a wife to periodically also refresh her perspective on marriage. A few minutes of reading a book such as this one or any of the other excellent marriage books out there, even once a week, will help keep her focused on how important it is to do all that is in her power to maintain shalom bayis.

Maybe she's being a bit too edgy, or perhaps she is expecting too much of her spouse. Perhaps she's not as attentive as she should be when he speaks or isn't putting enough effort into her appearance. Whatever it is, a few minutes of reading can go a long way toward helping reset her enthusiasm for her marriage and shalom bayis.

An excellent time for this is on Friday night when the men go to shul. Spending ten minutes — even five —will help her see that there are areas that, even if basically OK, could nevertheless be upgraded a bit.

I can't emphasize enough how much such a small investment of time can work wonders for a marriage. And, as someone once said to me after offering some much-needed advice, "Don't think about it; do it." Please. You won't regret it.

CHAPTER 17

Miscellaneous

In this section I will mention a few ideas regarding things that a wife should or should not do if she wants to maintain good shalom bayis. I will not elaborate on the whys; most of what I say here is self-explanatory.

1. Don't do for others what you won't do for him. This can get men very upset.

2. Don't ask him too often to do something because "I'm not dressed." Being asked to run out of the house due to you being in a house robe makes him feel that if you would have changed earlier he would not have to be doing this. Once in while is OK, but it shouldn't be a regular occurrence.

3. Don't throw away or rearrange the papers and things in his drawers without his express permission. This includes ties and other items of clothing that he may have a special affinity for. You can certainly tell him to get rid of something that you don't like, but don't take action unilaterally.

4. Don't ask him to do things that he finds particularly frustrating, like fixing things if he's not good with his hands or babysitting for extended periods of time. Frequent visits to family members or friends whom he finds particularly tiresome or annoying should also be avoided as much as possible.

5. Don't ever compare him to other men.

6. Don't ask or bring up anything about past relationships that either of you have been involved in, if that has been the case.

7. Don't say, "I let you learn for an hour; now you have to help me with the kids." This makes it sound like the learning is his fun and that you have less appreciation for Torah than you likely do. You could say, "I'd love for you to learn more, but I really need help just now."

8. Don't ever say anything deprecating about his parents or family members. The only exception would be if one of them has wronged you and you have to discuss with your husband how to deal with it.

9. Don't spend money irresponsibly.

10. Don't make a big deal out of little things.

I hope you have found this book helpful. I conclude with a *brachah* that you should have shalom bayis always.

Feel free to email me with questions at
Dovidbkaplan@gmail.com

My Wife, My Queen

A No-Holds-Barred *Shalom Bayis* Book for Men

DOVID KAPLAN

ADIR PRESS